ORIGAMI
DINOSAURS

by David Roberts
Illustrated by Leslie Caswell
Models by Brian Edwards

MALLARD
PRESS

STEGOSAURUS

About 120 million years ago, when the world began to cool down, the giant dinosaurs began to disappear and were replaced by new kinds of dinosaurs. One of the earliest of these dinosurs was Stegosaurus, or "plated lizard." It was protected from its enemies by

two rows of stiff armor plates that stood up along the high-curved, 30-foot length of its back. Each plate was covered with tough skin. These were a protection from the bite of the jaws of its enemies.

Stegosaurus was built for defense rather than attack and was entirely vegetarian. Its parrot-beak mouth was developed for tearing leaves and its teeth for grinding food, not tearing flesh.

TYLOSAURUS

Fish were the first of all living creatures to have skeletons made of bone. During the millions of years of evolution, some of these fish grew lungs for breathing air. They could then crawl ashore and begin to adapt themselves to life on land.

Some species found they could no longer compete with other land animals and returned to the water. There food was abundant and their enemies could not follow them.

One of these species was Tylosaurus, whose huge jaws were filled with razor-sharp teeth. The female continued to lay her

eggs on the shore, but the variety of fish in the sea provided a plentiful and easily-gathered food supply.

Tylosaurus developed a long tail to propel itself through the water and flippers for balance and changing direction. In the sea, it prospered and grew into a 20-foot monster.

TRICERATOPS

One of the most formidable of the armored dinosaurs living about 100 million years ago was Triceratops, or "three-horn-face." This creature was the ancestor of the modern rhinoceros, but was bigger and better equipped for both attack and defense.

From nose to tail, it was between 20 and 30 feet long. Behind its head was a towering, bony frill protecting the neck. Its skull was mounted on a ball-and-socket joint that allowed Triceratops to swiftly turn its three horns to face an enemy. It could charge with all the force of a bulldozer.

It was entirely vegetarian, its parrot-beak mouth adapted purely for tearing leaves from plants and trees. It had a small brain and was slow-thinking, but it was a strong opponent under attack.

PTERANODON

About 150 million years ago, some reptiles developed the

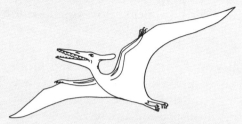

power of flight. Most of the early flying reptiles, called Pterosaurs, were more like bats. Instead of rows of feathers on their wings, they had a leathery skin.

These first flying reptiles were quite small, not much bigger than a pigeon. But by about 70 million years ago, Pteranodon, or "toothless wing," had developed a wing span of 20 feet.

Pteranodon would launch itself from a tree or a clifftop to soar out over the sea. Its sharp eyes would pick out a fish in the water, and it would dive down to snatch the fish in its long, pointed beak.

Caught on the ground, Pteranodon was easy prey to its enemies, the flesh-eating hunters. Its descendants, the bats, had to develop into much smaller flying creatures, venturing out mainly at night to hunt for food and hiding in caves during the day.

CORYTHOSAURUS

For well over 100 million years dinosaurs survived on the Earth. During the long period of their existence, each species developed its own protection from its enemies.

Corythosaurus, the "helmet lizard," was a vegetarian. It had a mouth like a duck's bill, with row upon row of small, overlapping teeth to grind its food. Corythosaurus kept close to the water for fear of its enemies. Its webbed feet allowed it to move

across marshy ground without sinking into the mud and becoming trapped there.

The purpose of the crest on the top of Corythosaurus's head remains a mystery. It's possible the crest allowed the dinosaur to breath underwater or improved the sense of smell or amplified warning and mating calls.

ARCHELON

More than 200 million years ago, some of the air-breathing reptiles began to return to the sea seeking protection from their enemies as well as new sources of food.

One of these marine reptiles was Archelon, the "ruler turtle," whose broad body was over 12 feet across. Its parrot-beaked mouth closely resembled that of the great armored Triceratops, which were its contemporaries on land. It was adept at catching small fish but was itself prey to the Mosasaurs, like Tylosaurus, with their great crocodile jaws.

Perhaps Archelon became extinct because it never developed the hard shell of the modern

turtle. Yet its descendants, turtles, tortoises, and terrapins, with their protective shells, have survived almost unchanged in all parts of the world both on land and in water.

Hints on Folding

Separate the six origami sheets from the book along the left-hand edge of each model.
Always fold on a flat, smooth, and hard surface.

Make the folds as carefully as possible along the folding lines. Heavy black folding lines (--------) are always on the *INSIDE* of the fold. Sometimes a thin dotted line (........) shows where to make a fold and this may be on the outside.
Lightly press the fold, then check that it follows the folding line before pressing it down firmly with your fingernail.
As you make a fold, keep an eye on the drawing that follows it to make sure that each stage is right before starting the next one.

Each stage is numbered. Read the directions for each stage and be sure that you understand them before you make the fold on your model.

You will find a background on the inside front and back cover to use with your completed models. Once you have completed the models remove the staples from the middle of the book and remove the pages. The cover can then be propped upright.

Here is a simple folding test:

1. Take a square piece of paper and fold it in half.

2. Fold it again at an angle.

3. Straighten it out again and make the same fold to the other side of the paper.

4. Straighten this out and make another fold at a slightly different angle further along the paper. Straighten it out and make the same fold to the other side of the paper as you did before.

5. Straighten this fold out and hold the top corners with each hand.

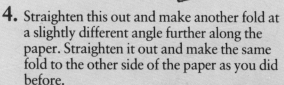
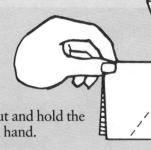

6. Open the paper out slightly and take the left corner down under the right one, as far as the second fold will allow.

7. Pull it forward again as far as the other fold will allow. This is the most difficult type of fold you will have to make with your origami models.

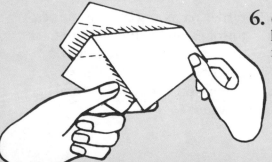
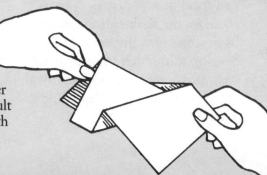

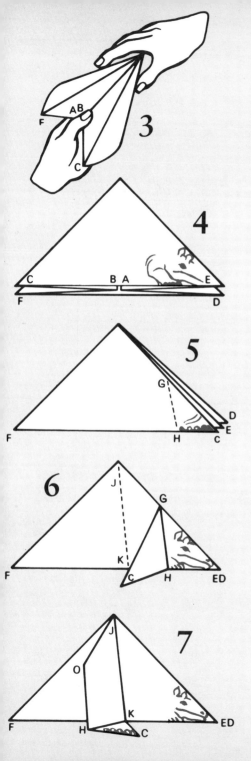

STEGOSAURUS

1. Lay the paper down with the eyes on top. Fold AB and then open out flat again.

2. Turn the paper over and fold CD. Open this out and do the same with EF. Open out flat again.

3. Take point B over to point A and hold them together in your left hand. Press the two sides together with your other hand.

4. This is how your Stegosaurus should look.

5. Fold flap C over top of E and D.

6. Fold C back again at line GH.

7. Without unfolding GH fold this flap over again at JH.

8. Turn the model over.

9. Fold flap D back, first at LM and again at JN, in the same way that you did on the other side.

10. Fold OR first to one side of the model, then to the other and then straighten it out again. Do the same with QR.

11. Now push point F back inside the model as far as OR will allow.

12. Pull F out again as far as QR will allow.

13. Fold ST, UT, WX and YX first to one side and then the other. Remember to straighten each one out before starting the next.

14. Push point E inside the model as far as ST will allow and pull it out again as far as UT will allow.

15. Do the same with WX and YX and finally tuck point E just inside the nose.

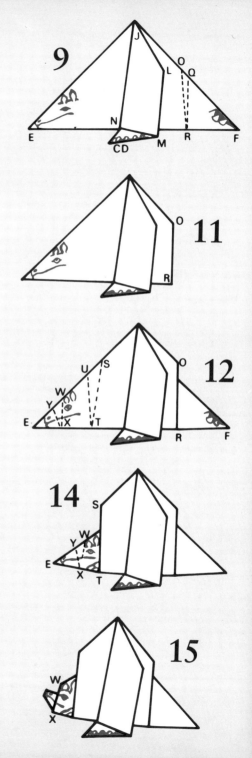

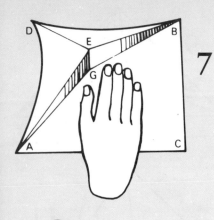

7

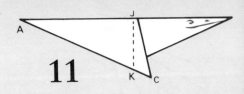

11

TYLOSAURUS

1. Fold AB and open out flat again.

2. Fold CD and open out flat again.

3. Fold AE and open out again. Try not to crease further than point E.

4. Do the same with BE, AF and BF.

5. Turn the paper over so that the eyes are on top.

6. Fold AH and open out flat. Do the same with AG, BG and BH.

7. Hold the middle of the paper down flat with one hand and make folds BE and AE stand up.

8. Squeeze fold DE by holding just behind point E with finger and thumb. Push E forwards and downwards.

9. Now make folds BF and AF stand up and bring point F over to meet E.

10. Fold flaps DE and FC down flat towards the head.

11. Fold AB.

12. Fold the flippers back on both sides at JK.

13. Fold LM first to one side of the model and then to the other. Straighten this out again. Do the same with NO.

14. Pull the head down as far as NO will allow so that part of it is inside the body. The head will now be inside out.

15. Pull the head up again as far as LM will allow.

16. Fold PQ and RS in the same way as you did the last folds.

17. Pull the tail down as far as PQ will allow and up again as far as RS, in the same way as the head.

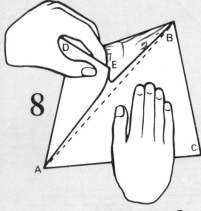

8

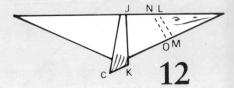

12

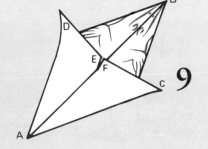

9

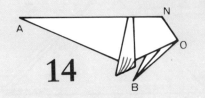

14

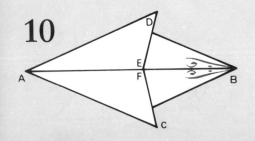

10

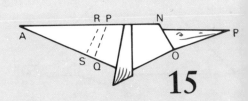

15

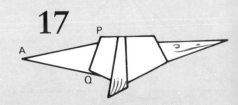

17

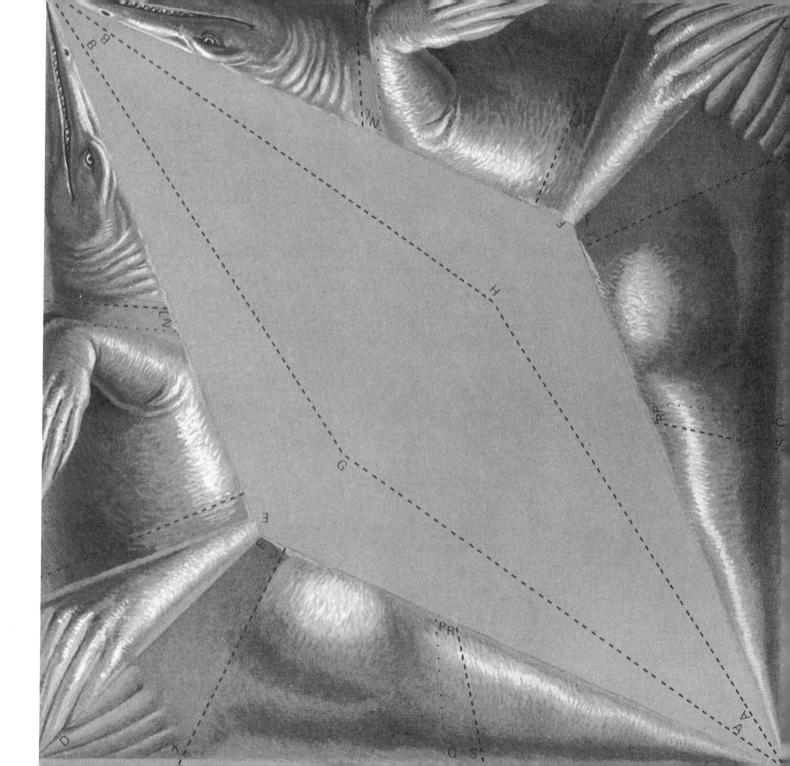

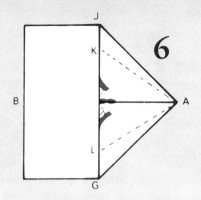

6

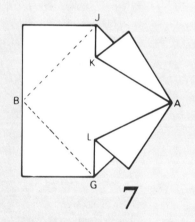

7

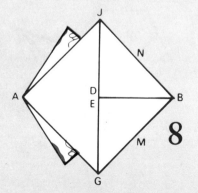

8

TRICERATOPS

1. Fold AB and open out flat again.
2. Fold CD and open out again. Try not to crease further than point C.
3. Fold CE and open out again.
4. Fold FG and open out. Do the same with FB. Try not to crease further than point F.
5. Fold HJ and open out and then do the same with HB.
6. Fold AJ and AG.
7. Fold KA and LA.
8. Turn the paper over and fold GB and BJ.
9. Take hold of point M and bend this downwards along GF and FB.
10. Do the same with point N.
11. Bring E and D together by pushing CB inwards. The back should be folded along CA.

Continued

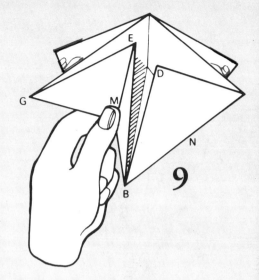

9

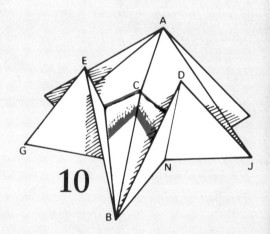

10

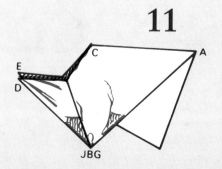

11

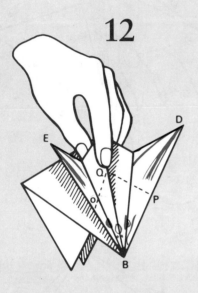

12

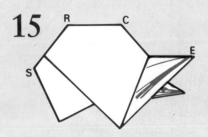

15

Triceratops continued

12. Hold point C with thumb and second finger of your left hand. Pull E and D apart with your other hand. Place your first finger on point Q and grip tightly.

13. Now lift point B and push QB upwards to form a ridge. Take your finger away from Q and bring E and D together again to make folds QO and QP.

14. Fold RS first to one side of the model and then to the other. Straighten this fold out again. Do the same with TU.

15. Push point A inside the model as far as RS will allow.

16. Pull A out again as far as TU will allow.

17. Form each horn at CV so that they point outwards at a slight angle and fold the back feet up at WX.

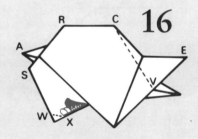

16

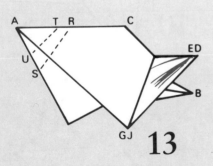

13

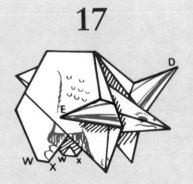

17

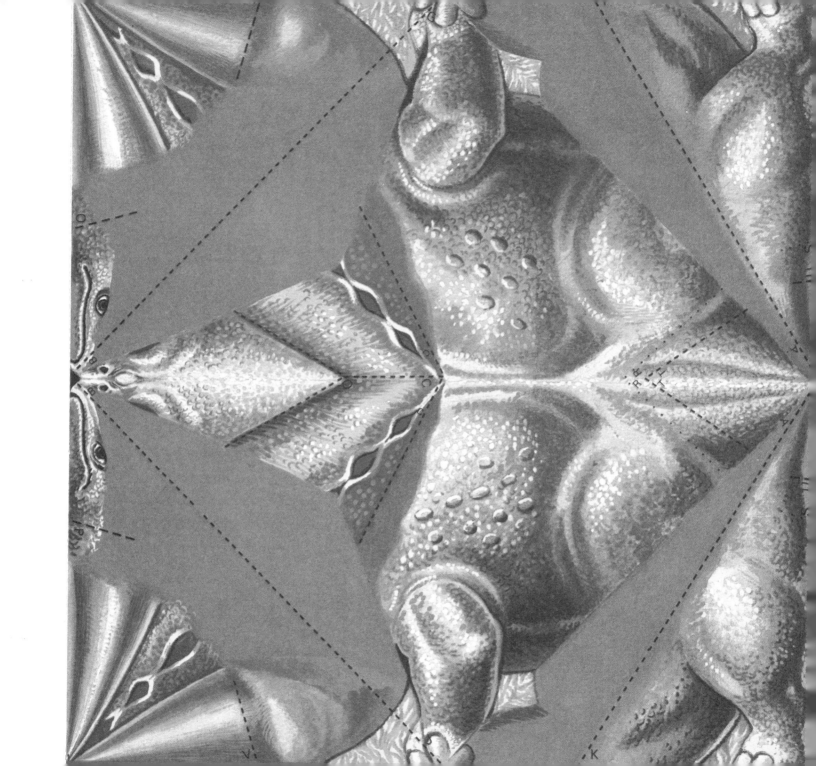

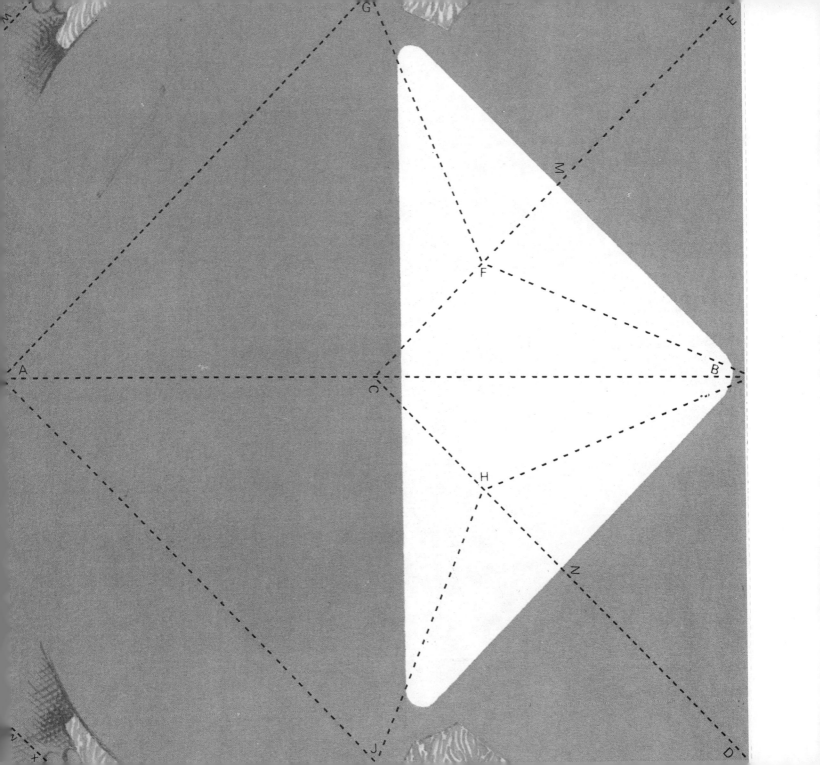

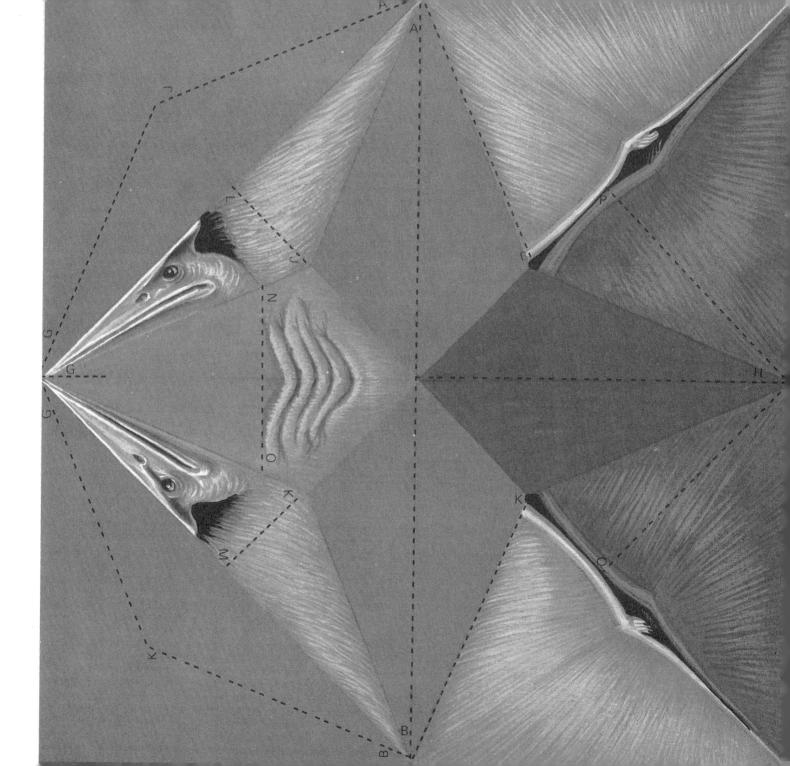

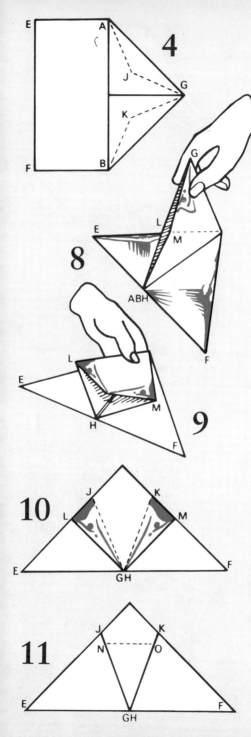

PTERANODON

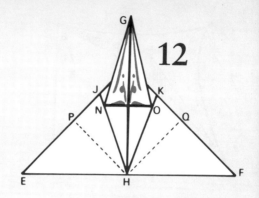

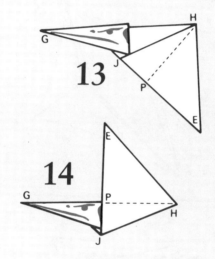

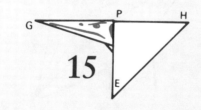

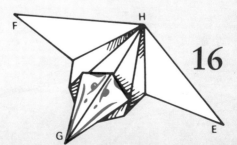

1. Lay the paper down with the eyes on top. Fold AB and open out flat again.

2. Turn the paper over so that the eyes are underneath. Fold GH and open out flat.

3. Fold DE and open out again. Do the same with CF.

4. Fold AG and BG.

5. Pick up point B and fold KG, then open this out again. Try not to crease the paper further than point K.

6. Pick up G and fold BK, then open the fold out again.

7. In the same way fold AJ and JG.

8. Take point A over to point H and then B over to H, so that G is standing upright.

9. Push point G down to point H, at the same time make sure than L and M are pulled outwards.

10. This is how it should look from above.

11. Lift G up a little way and push point L inside the model as far as fold JG will allow. Do the same with point M.

12. Fold NO by taking point G over to the top.

13. Fold the Pteranodon in half along GH.

14. Fold the wings up at JH and KH.

15. Fold them down again at PH and QH.

16. Now pull the wing-tips apart so that the model looks like this.

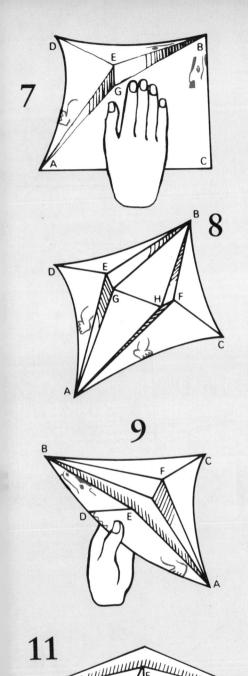

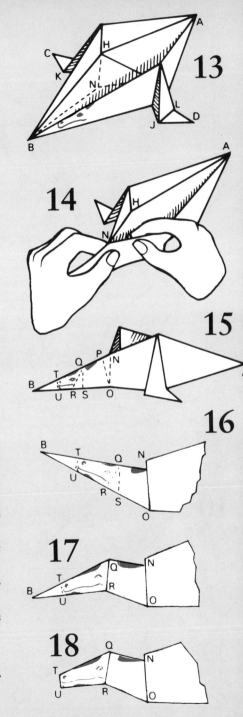

CORYTHOSAURUS

1. Fold AB and open out flat again.

2. Fold CD and open out flat again.

3. Fold AE and open out again. Try not to crease further than point E.

4. Do the same with BE, AF and BF.

5. Turn the paper over so that the eyes are on top.

6. Fold AH and open out flat. Do the same with AG, BG and BH.

7. Hold the middle of the paper down flat with one hand and make folds BE and AE stand up.

8. Do the same with folds AF and BF.

9. Squeeze fold DE with finger and thumb and fold the whole of this flap forward so that D points towards B.

10. Squeeze FC and fold C forwards towards B.

11. Fold point D back again along EJ.

12. Do the same on the other side at FK.

13. Fold D and C outwards at JL and KM.

14. From inside the model push the neck upwards at point N and squeeze the sides together. With finger and thumb carefully crease along NH and NG.

15. Fold the neck at NO by folding first to one side of the model and then to the other. Straighten out and do the same with PO, QS, QR and TU.

16. Open out model across the neck and push folds PO inside folds NO.

17. Push folds QS inside folds QR.

18. Tuck point B inside the head by folding at TU.

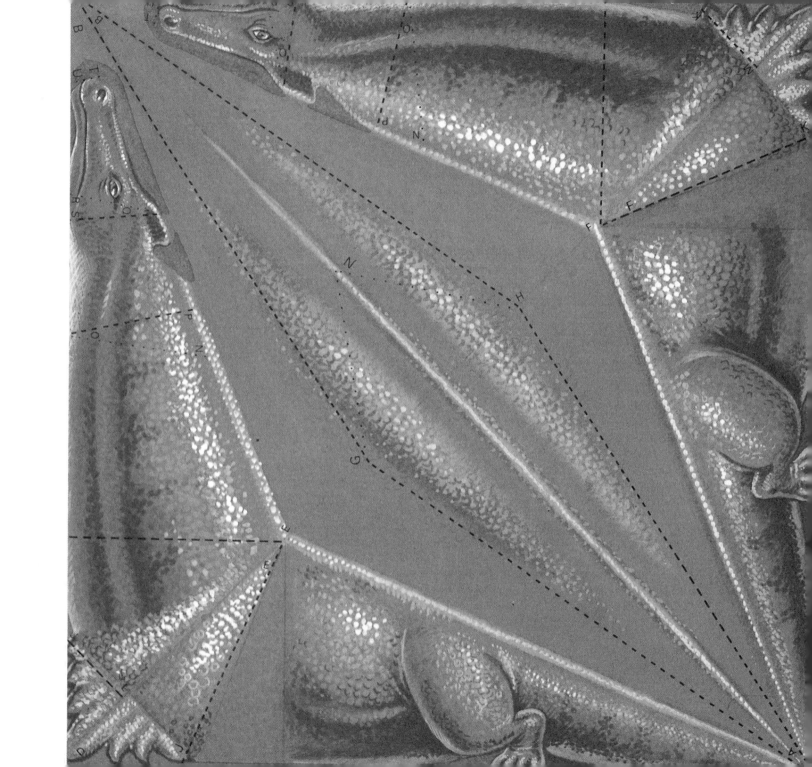

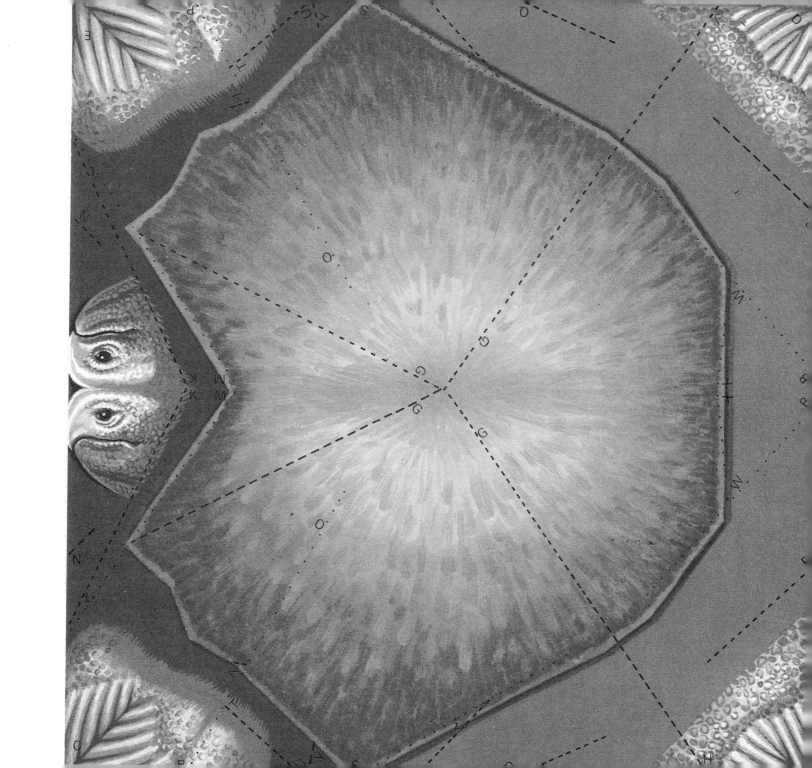

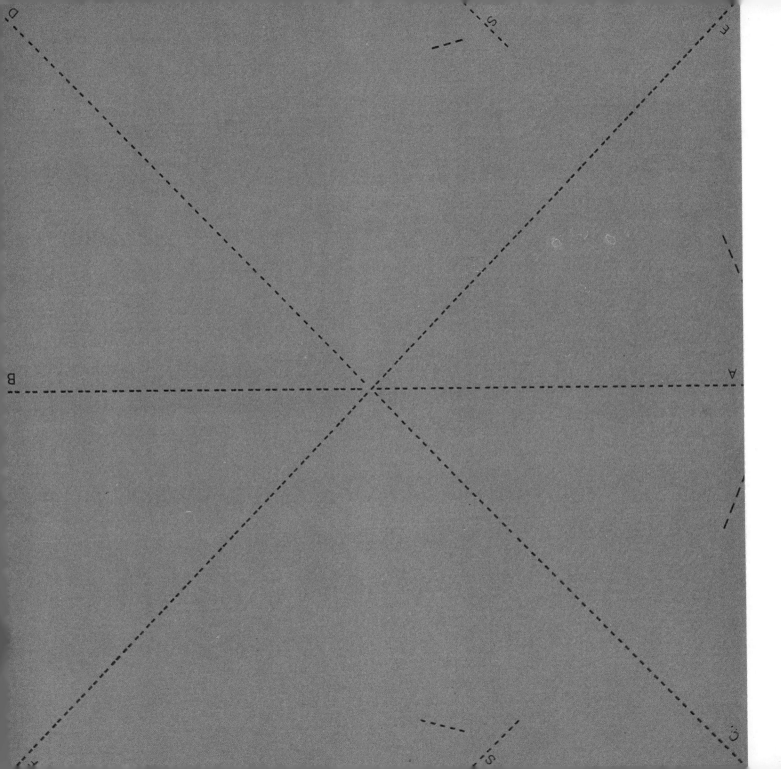

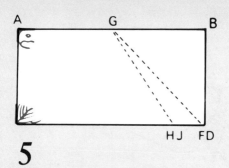

5

ARCHELON

1. Fold CD and open out flat again.

2. Do the same with EF.

3. Lay the paper with the eyes on top and fold GH. Try not to crease further than point G. Open out flat again

4. Do the same with GJ.

5. Turn the paper over and fold AB.

6. Push GH and GJ inside the model as far as GF and GD will allow. Both GF and GD will be on the outside of the model.

7. Fold ML first to one side and then to the other. Straighten out again. Do the same with KL.

8. Push point A inside the model as far as ML will allow. The head will now be inside out.

9. Pull point A out again as far as KL will allow.

10. Fold GN first to one side and then to the other. Straighten this out again.

11. Push GN down inside the model as far as GC and GE will allow.

12. Fold both front legs inwards at OP.

Continued

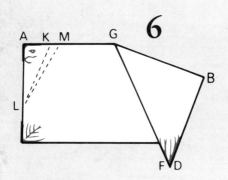

6

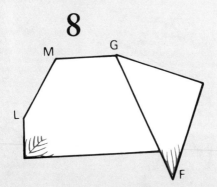

8

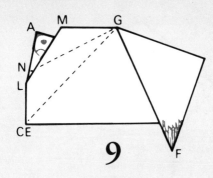

9

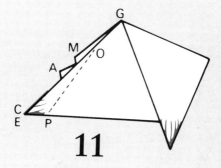

11

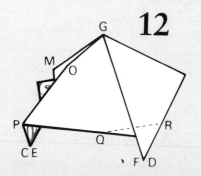

12

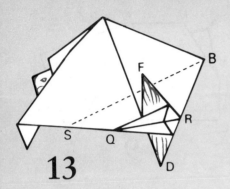

13

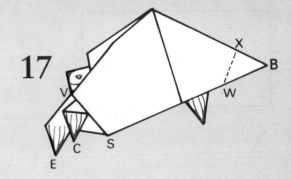

17

Archelon continued

13. Fold F up at QR.

14. Tuck QR up inside the Archelon by folding BS.

15. Repeat the last two stages with the back leg on the other side.

16. Fold the front leg up at TU.

17. Tuck TU up inside the model by folding at VS. Look inside the front leg for this fold.

18. Do the same with the other front leg.

19. Fold WX first to one side of the model and then to the other. Straighten this fold and push B up inside the shell as far as WX will allow.

20. Tuck the side flaps up into the Archelon at YZ. This is shown on the inside of the shell.

21. Bend each foot outwards a little way and pull the two sides of the shell slightly apart.

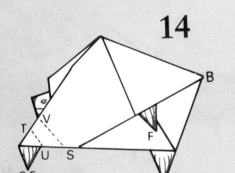

14

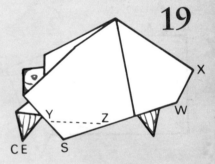

19

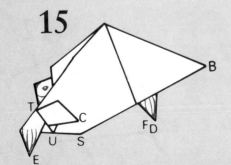

15

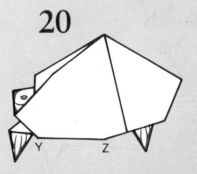

20